Washington Monument, 1945

BODINE'S BALTIMORE

Shot Tower, Fayette and Front Streets, 1924

BODINE'S BALTIMORE

46 YEARS IN THE LIFE OF A CITY

Photographs by A. Aubrey Bodine
F.P.S.A. and F.N.P.P.

Commentary by Wilbur Harvey Hunter
Director of the Peale Museum

Foreword by Harold A. Williams

Published by Bodine & Associates, Inc.
Baltimore, Maryland

OTHER BOOKS BY
A. AUBREY BODINE

"My Maryland"
"The Face of Maryland"
"Chesapeake Bay and Tidewater"
"The Face of Virginia"
"Baltimore Today"

First Edition
Library of Congress
   Catalog No. 72-133334
SBN 0-910254-2
Copyright 1973 by
   Bodine & Associates, Inc.
Printed in the U.S.A.

Watermelon Man, East Montgomery Street, 1930's

CONTENTS

Foreword by Harold A. Williams	vi
Introduction: "Bodine's Baltimore" by Wilbur Harvey Hunter	viii
ONE: The Pace was Gentler	2
The Old Harbor	4
Markets in the Streets	11
Neighborhoods in the 1930's	13
The Old Suburbs	18
Downtown	20
Vanished Landmarks	22
Fun and Games: The Park	26
Playgrounds	28
Swimming Holes	29
Excursions	30
Changing Baltimore	34
TWO: The Great War	39
Off to the Wars	42
On the Home Front	44
All Over	48
THREE: The Big Scene	50
The Street Scene	61
Markets, downtown, neighborhoods	
The Players	78
Featured Players	90
Scholars and Their Schools	104
Festivals	120
The Sport of Kings	124
Sports for Everyone	130
The New Baltimore	137
Index	148

FOREWORD

A. Aubrey Bodine loved Baltimore. To him it was a unique and charming commingling of a bustling metropolis with old-fashioned traditions, ancient beauty and picturesque ways.

Most of all he loved the charm and quaintness of the city, particularly the city of his youth, which was Baltimore in the Twenties and Thirties—the Bay steamers shuttling in and out of the Pratt and Light street wharves, the beauty of Mount Vernon Place at dusk, streetcars swaying and clanking across the Guilford avenue trestle, sheep grazing on the slopes of the Mansion House lawn in Druid Hill Park, bugeyes and skipjacks from the Shore piled high with watermelons at Long Dock.

He was not a civic booster in the usual sense, but he had an immense pride in Baltimore and its accomplishments. He was proud of the fact that the Johns Hopkins Hospital was internationally known, that the Bethlehem Steel plant was the largest in the world, that Baltimore was once the straw hat capital, and that ships from all over the world—from Rotterdam, Cape Town, Yokohama—brought their cargoes to Baltimore. He had an amazing knowledge of Baltimore. Some of this came from newspapers or books, but much of it was first hand information he acquired when he was on assignment. He had the innate curiosity of a good reporter and knew how to get information.

When he was producing one of his books he provided the caption writer with a stream of statistics and information which he insisted be used. In his book, "Chesapeake Bay and Tidewater," for example, he had the writer include such superlative statements as "Baltimore, in addition to being the nation's chief metallic ore import center is also the leading East Coast port for grain, fertilizer and chemicals" and "Baltimore is the largest port in the world for Volkswagen entries." And, one of my favorites because it reveals so much about the lengths he would go to for the right picture (this in his own words)—"This is the third time this flag has flown over Fort McHenry. The reason is for lack of manpower. For this view, it required the entire staff at Fort McHenry along with the assistance of ten Coast Guardsmen to hoist it properly. The weight and size of this fifteen star flag is enormous. It measures 30 x 42 feet in size. After it has been raised the staff must watch it like a hawk, for a breeze livelier than twenty knots will very likely tear the flag to shreds."

He had a proprietary interest in the city and he would never take what he considered an unfavorable picture of it. When he saw something that he thought could be improved he wrote the mayor or whoever he thought could help. In a letter to the chairman of the board of the First National Bank some years ago he declared, "Around the corner from my home is a group of interesting old houses which I am told belong to your bank. They have just been painted a very attractive brick red with a coat of green on the woodwork which is a pleasant departure from the conventional white or cream. My suggestion is that the painters leave well enough alone and do not ruin the appearance by putting white stripes over the brick to indicate mortar. The stripe painting seems to be an ancient custom in Baltimore, but they give a false appearance and fade in a month or so, this giving a shabby appearance." One development that annoyed him more than stripe painting was the widespread use of artificial stone covering on rowhouses. Whenever he drove through East Baltimore he would rage that the beauty of these houses had been destroyed by home improvement companies.

U. S. F. Constitution, Recreation Pier, 1933

He usually had one or two private campaigns going to preserve an ancient landmark, restore an old building or add trees to a public square. When he was commissioned to illustrate an article about Baltimore for *Holiday* magazine he saw it first and foremost as an opportunity to display the glories and charm of the city. He was generous in lending or giving pictures to publications that promoted the city. For years he provided the cover picture for *Baltimore*, the magazine published by the Chamber of Commerce of Metropolitan Baltimore.

For most of his life he lived in the center of the city. For years his home was at 805 Park Avenue, across the street from the First Presbyterian Church which he said had one of the most beautiful spires he had ever photographed. His home was filled with Maryland and Baltimore items, including a fine collection of books. The window screens of his house were painted with Baltimore scenes, copied from his photographs, by William A. Oktavec, the East Baltimore screen painter. In his backyard were a wooden barber pole (the last one in town, he claimed) and a street gas lamp he had acquired from the municipality.

Bodine had a unique knowledge of the city which was a result of personal and professional interests. He knew where the last cobblestone alleys were, the blocks where one could find two or three busybodies (a device used in the old days to observe the street and front steps from an upstairs window), and the streets in Fells Point where wooden steps were overturned at night by the householders to signify that they had retired.

He took great delight in searching out the best places for common or uncommon services. He advised his friends where old time craftsmen still plied their trade, where to have knives sharpened, jewelry repaired, antique furniture restored and suits rewoven (as a pipe smoker he often burned holes in his jackets and slacks). He considered himself an authority on restaurants. Marconi's was his favorite, but he also enjoyed patronizing small, out-of-the-way places usually known only in their immediate neighborhoods.

The Baltimore Bodine knew and loved was rapidly disappearing, or had already disappeared, when he died in the fall of 1970. But because of his knowledge and love of Baltimore, much of what it was between 1924 and 1970—the years he worked as a photographer for the *Sunday Sun*—has been preserved in his photographs.

HAROLD A. WILLIAMS

BODINE'S BALTIMORE

46 YEARS IN THE LIFE OF A CITY

This is the panorama of a generation through photographs made by A. Aubrey Bodine between 1924 and 1970. A staff photographer for the *Sunday Sun* all those years, and latterly almost an institution in himself, he took many thousands of pictures of newsworthy people, buildings, streets, ships and all sorts of activities from the ordinary to the remarkable. From this enormous stockpile I have chosen those which seem most interesting as we look back on the record of this generation, particularly pictures of people, how they worked, their neighborhoods, the games they played, and things which influenced their lives. It is not a book about architecture or famous people or great events or even history in the formal sense, but a personal commentary on 46 years of life in Baltimore.

Aubrey Bodine published a number of photographic books dealing with the Chesapeake Bay region, Virginia and Maryland, and Harold A. Williams summed up his career in the 1971 biography, *Bodine: A Legend in His Time*. However, in his own books Bodine used up-to-date pictures for most topics while the biography dwelt on his salon photographs. None of them covered the historical ground I have attempted. In fact, only fifteen of the photographs in this book appeared in any of the others, and a large number were not even published in the newspapers.

The opportunity to investigate the full scope of his work came when Mrs. Bodine deposited about fifteen thousand of his negatives in the Peale Museum in 1971. The artist had already given the museum several thousand of his earliest negatives, many of them glass plates from the 1920s and 1930s. As we sorted and indexed these pictures the idea for a historical review of modern Baltimore emerged—a kind of family album of a generation of Baltimoreans by a man who knew and loved the city better than most, and had both the time and talent to make superb photographs. As a historian of Baltimore, and a resident for most of the same period, I conceived this book as a sort of collaboration in which Bodine's life work and my own merged.

As might be expected, the pictures have different meanings for me than for Bodine. Some that

East from Federal Hill, June 29, 1929

he made on routine assignments, and little regarded, are now of the greatest interest, while his highly finished salon photographs are not always relevant to history. Aubrey Bodine did not set out to record history but to photograph the current scene. Time has proved that much of what he did is indeed of historical quality because he was not merely an amateur following a hobby but a professional whose work took him to places and among people of great significance. Fortunately for us, he also had the enthusiasm and curiosity of an informed amateur and poked around in the odd corners of Baltimore for unusual material, and made a special point of recording street scenes and picturesque details which he thought were likely to change soon.

In planning the book there were a number of curious problems. The quantity of material was sometimes embarrassing—which of the several hundred pictures of the Flower Mart to choose? Then, there were disconcerting gaps in the historical coverage—nothing pertinent to the Depression, almost nothing on football and baseball, no pictures of such famous places as Miller Brothers or the Hotel Rennert, and so on. It was not easy to identify the pictures we did have. Bodine often filed his negatives according to a personal and arbitrary system, and the pencil notes on the negative envelopes seldom gave more than place, name and date, and usually less information than that. Often there was nothing at all, or worse, a cryptic word which might turn out to be misspelled anyway. Deduction and plain guesswork got us most of the answers but not all, and some pictures have been used because of their inherent pictorial interest although we did not know all the details.

The book's argument comes down to this: A. Aubrey Bodine was one of the generation which began in the days of sailing ships, horse drawn wagons and electric street cars and came to know jet planes, the expressway and nuclear power. I have tried to illustrate the life style of that generation in Baltimore with his pictures and my commentary.

WILBUR HARVEY HUNTER
Director, The Peale Museum

Fishing for gudgeon, Patapsco River, 1930's

1700 block Thames Street, 1935

Cathedral, Palm Sunday, March 29, 1942

"Two and a quarter centuries after their founding, some Maryland settlements have disappeared entirely, some remain small and quaint and flavorous of those days long gone, some others have grown moderately. But Baltimore, since 1729, has forged its way high up in the ranks of the nation's great cities and today presents to the eye, and the imagination, an endless array of colorful and contrasting facets.

Bright facets, too; so bright that many a one is sufficient in itself to hold the gaze. Thus some beholders see only the vast and throbbing world port, others only the hallowed patriotic shrine, the world-renowned medical and educational center, or the museums and schools devoted to the fine arts, and so on. Still others, limited to a quick glance, remember the city ever afterward for its famous rows of gleaming white steps, or the countless statues and other monuments that dot its streets and parks and bring it the nickname of Monumental City.

All of these facets catch the eye of the photographer, too, and all are represented on the pages that follow. But as he explores the city's odd corners and byways, the photographer comes upon many things that are less conspicuous, but no less interesting and no less characteristic of his Baltimore. And so pictures of these things, too, will be found.

There are, for instance, some steps that should be as famous as the white ones—the wooden steps of Fountain Street that are turned upside down, or even taken indoors, when the home-owner wishes to discourage callers. There are such picturesque scenes as a downtown street on a snowy night, and that created by a house that is simply covered with elaborate grillwork. All details in the great panorama of present-day Baltimore, but all fascinating details of—My Baltimore."

A. AUBREY BODINE "My Maryland", 1952

Skinny dipping, Patapsco River

ONE

THE PACE WAS GENTLER

When A. Aubrey Bodine photographed the Shot Tower in 1924 the Model T was Baltimore's most popular car, but there were still almost as many horse-drawn wagons as automobiles, and mass public transportation meant the electric trolley car. Most of the 800,000 Baltimore residents lived near the central business district in modest brick houses built compactly row after row, each with its postage stamp-sized backyard.

Neighborhood meant something in the 1920's. Although physically submerged in the city's mass the ancient historical settlements such as Fell's Point, Old Town, Waverly, Irvington and Franklintown still had sentimental identities, just as Baltimoreans still spoke of the "Marsh Market," at Market Space where there had been no marsh for more than a century. Other neighborhoods derived their identities from a public square such as Franklin, Union or Lafayette or one of the eight or ten public markets, or sometimes an ethnic tradition. The vicinity of Hollins Market was still considered to be an "Irish" political ward. There were a good many descendants of German immigrants around Union and Franklin Squares, and out Harford Road. In the Broadway area and along Eastern Avenue were recent immigrants from Poland and

Druid Hill Boat Lake in winter

old Bohemia, while Orthodox Jews from Eastern Europe clustered near Lloyd and Lombard Streets where there were a number of synagogues and *kosher* food stores. "Little Italy" was an enclave of houses, restaurants and stores genuinely reflecting the needs of the immigrant residents. And, throughout the city were well-defined neighborhoods of black people. It was still a common experience to grow up, attend school and church and marry within the neighborhood in which you were born. Conversely, a visit "downtown" was a considerable expedition, not taken lightly or forgotten soon.

Life seemed to have a gentler pace in those days. Adventurous youngsters went "skinny-dipping" in the yet-unpolluted rivers, and the city streets were the common playgrounds, automobiles being only occasional interruptions to the games. Druid Hill Park, and the other parks, were recreation facilities for the whole population, much used winter and summer, and for a special big family treat there were excursions by steamboat to Betterton or Tolchester. Oyster roasts, crab feasts and neighborhood festivals were important social occasions—ambitious politicians attended every one.

Although Baltimore appeared to be standing still in the 20's and 30's, there were changes underway foreshadowing the dislocations of city life in our times—automobiles increased in number, suburbs spread further and further out and attracted residents from the inner city, and the airplane challenged the railroad for passengers. The city was growing up faster than we knew.

THE BUSIEST CORNER IN BALTIMORE

In Bodine's 1930s photograph from the top of our first "skyscraper," the newly completed Baltimore Trust Building (now Maryland National Bank), the old inner harbor looks little different from its appearance in Civil War days. It was still the terminus for a fleet of white Chesapeake Bay steam packet boats which linked Baltimore with Richmond, Norfolk, Crisfield, Annapolis, Easton, Wilmington, Philadelphia and points between— a dozen boats are shown nestled in their slips along Light Street. The busiest corner in Baltimore *(above)* was the crossing of Pratt and Light Streets with its clattering mixture of horse drawn wagons, trucks, motorcycles, street cars and mounted police. Here and in only a few other places in the city, a policeman was stationed at the intersection in an elevated kiosk to direct traffic with a hand-operated stop-and-go signal. Dodging other vehicles and the traffic kiosk was only part of the driving adventure at this corner—the narrow tires and two-wheel brakes of the 1930 automobiles made the slippery stone paving and railroad tracks unpredictable hazards.

THE WATERMELON FLEET IS IN!

Pier 4, at the foot of the "Marsh" Market Space, was the haven for a fleet of skipjacks, bugeyes and other Chesapeake Bay sailing craft bringing fresh produce, fish, crabs, and oysters from dozens of small ports around the Bay to Baltimore. Wholesalers and retailers met the boats to bargain for a truck load or a bushel. To small boys the watermelon season was special, and they gathered at dockside, hoping for a piece from a broken melon. Has it ever tasted so good since?

The longshoreman, that everyday Atlas, did much of the port's work in the 1930s with his strong back and sturdy legs. The white "banana boat" which docked in the inner harbor carried a glamorous cargo. It brought visions of romantic Caribbean islands and tropical jungles, and indeed, every so often some tropical fauna—snakes and spiders—in the bunches of bananas.

Thomas Kensett perfected the technique for preserving fruits and vegetables in sealed "cans" in Baltimore in the 1850s, and the city was still a national leader of food processing in the 1930s. Local specialties were sugar corn and tomatoes brought in by boat to the canneries in Canton.

The great wholesale produce markets were at the "Marsh" Market Space *(above)* and along Light and Charles Streets below Pratt *(below)*. Bustling from midnight to early morning supplying hotels, restaurants and grocers, the business was largely over by noon and the markets became strangely deserted.

NEIGHBORHOODS IN THE 1930's

Nearly every inner city neighborhood had its own shopping center, a public market. In season, farmers and hucksters set up stalls outside the market along nearby streets. Hollins Market *(left)* had five blocks of street stalls along Hollins Street from Carey to Poppleton in 1929. Broadway Market *(below)* spanned three blocks from Eastern Avenue down to Thames Street with every inside stall occupied and some street booths. There was no need for parking lots. The customers came by foot or street car, rarely by automobile.

Each downtown neighborhood had Bureau of Street Cleaning men working regular beats with shovel, broom and two-wheeled cart—called the "Hokey Cart." In the 1930s there weren't very many parked cars in the way of a clean sweep.

Franklin Square *(below)*, dedicated 1839, is one of the nine old residential squares of the inner city, each one a true neighborhood oasis. The others are Union, Harlem Park, Lafayette, Perkins Spring, Madison, Johnson, Collington, and the best-known, Mount Vernon Place. For games the streets were more fun than playgrounds —"Ring-around-a-rosie" in mother's shoes.

(left) Stoop sitting on one of the back streets in East Baltimore.
(above) In the heart of Little Italy: St. Leo's carnival on Exeter Street in the 30s.
(below) Kosher live poultry market on East Lombard Street near Lloyd.

THE OLD SUBURBS

(left above) Dickeyville, 1934
(left below) Roland Park, 1941

Old U.S. Arsenal in Pikesville in 1932 when it was the Maryland Line Confederate Soldiers Home. It is now the headquarters of the Maryland State Police.

DOWNTOWN

In the 1930s downtown was the place for important shopping, and a full excursion included rambling through all the big stores, luncheon at a tea room or soda fountain, and a matinee at one of the flamboyantly decorated movie "palaces," such as the Century or Valencia on Lexington Street, all gold and velvet and glitter.
(above) Lexington Street at Liberty. *(below)* Baltimore at Charles Street.

Waiting for the street car . . .

Here comes the snow plow . . .

At last, the car.

VANISHED LANDMARKS

(left) East Pleasant Street in 1930, a group of charming houses already a century old. The one at the left was Baltimore's first gallery for "modern" art, sponsored by a citizens' group called the Friends of Art.

(above) The town residence of Johns Hopkins until his death in 1873 at 18 West Saratoga Street —demolished in 1931, it is a parking lot today.

(below) Ezekiel Towson's Tavern, York Road, was a coach and wagon stop since the 1790s and the nucleus of the town which became the burgeoning county seat of today. It was demolished in 1929.

Number 1 street car line from Roland Park came down Guilford Avenue on an overhead trestle starting at Biddle Street and coming to earth at Lexington Street by the City Hall. The scenic nine-block elevated ride had two stations, one of which was opposite the City Jail.

To build a new central facility for the Enoch Pratt Free Library, a block of fine old town houses on Cathedral Street was demolished. *(above)* Mayor Howard W. Jackson laid the cornerstone of the new building January 12, 1932. One year later the books were moved in and the "Main Branch," as Baltimoreans always call it, was then open for business.

Baltimore's greatest playground, winter or summer, was Druid Hill Park (often pronounced *Droodle*). The boat lake was a splendid ice rink, or in the summer, fine for fishing and boating—there are no boats now, and the lake is used for the Zoo's waterfowl exhibit. Mansion House hill drew admirers, summer and winter. In the late 30s the Zoo's prize elephant, Minnie, put on a Sunday show worthy of the circus.

Playtime for children in the 1930s could be as simple as the sliding board and merry-go-round, or as glamorous as a visit to Carlin's Amusement Park at Park Circle with its racer dip, Fun House, and many other things to delight and excite.

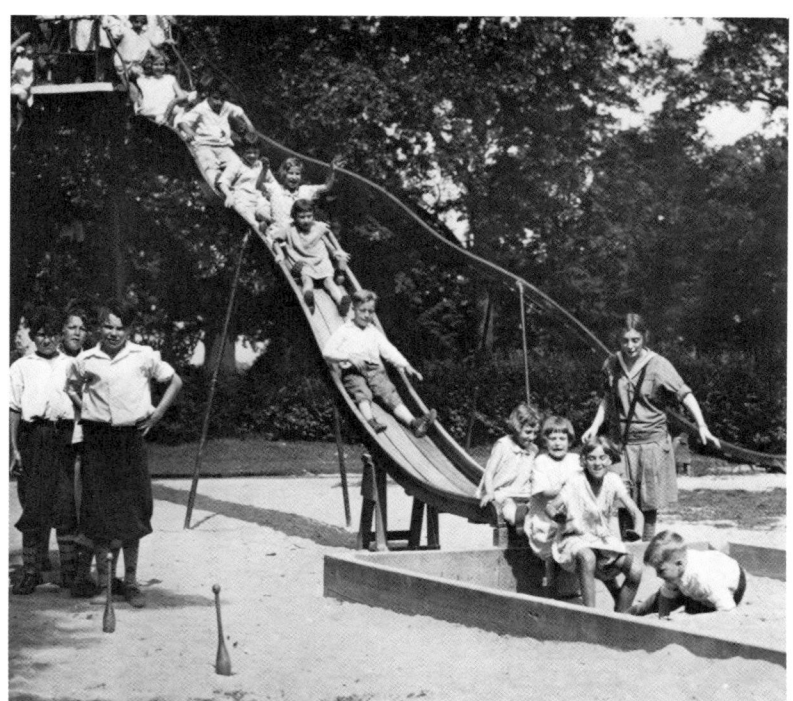

The daredevil teen-age crowd of the 30s liked swimming in the icy waters of the Beaver Dam Quarries near Cockeysville which was both dangerous and unchaperoned. *(below)* The less adventurous puddled around Clifton Park's vast public pool which was as safe as a bath tub and often just as warm.

For many, the high point of the summer in the 1930s would be a day excursion to Betterton *(above)* or Tolchester *(middle)* on the Eastern Shore. Getting there on such steam boats as the *Louise, Emma Giles,* and *Bay Belle* was half the fun. Another seasonal event *(below)* was the gudgeon run up the Patapsco in the spring. Not much as food, they were easy to catch even for youngsters.

Baltimore had social clubs without number. *(top)* In 1930 this crowd dressed like farmers and made a big show of drinking "naturally fermented" cider in defiance of the law—the Prohibition law, that is. Three years later "the noble experiment" was repealed and all the clubs drank to that. *(below)* A traditional feature in many club outings was the Rivers Chambers Orchestra which knew all the good old music and a few exotic ballads, too. They are about to embark for the 1940 Bar Association annual cruise.

The German immigration of the early 1800s left a strong impression on Baltimore. Socially, it was expressed in festive outings to nearby beer gardens which featured choral singing, dancing to accordion bands, target shooting, and of course, beer. This one was in 1938.

Oysters by the barrel and beer by the keg were the ingredients of the traditional Baltimore political outing in the "R" months. Opening oysters was a feat of manual dexterity not easily learned without pain—eating the juicy bivalve off the half shell was a test of gracefulness.

Like a herd of monsters looming out of the primeval mists, the locomotives at the Orangeville yard in 1929 exude a sense of power and danger, too. *(below)* Spouting like some great whale, the Fireboat *Torrent* moves in a shimmering panoply of spray. *(right)* Bodine leaned out of a window in the *Sun* Building to photograph this spectacular blaze on Redwood Street near Hanover in 1939.

The air age approached tentatively. Some favored the helium-filled dirigible. In 1931 the U.S. Navy Akron flew over the new Baltimore Trust Building—it was as large as the building—and crashed two years later. More successful were the Glenn L. Martin Company's big sea plane "Clippers" made on Middle River. This is #7, launched in 1936. Many Baltimoreans took their first air trip on a Clipper to Bermuda or the Caribbean, leaving from the municipal Harbor Field.

The Curtiss-Wright Airport *(above)* at Smith and Greenspring Avenues was for private flying, and in 1931 a monster air show of the latest planes. Shown is the fabled Ford Tri-Motor, nicknamed the "tin goose." *(below)* The city's first commercial passenger airport was the former U.S. Army Logan Field in Dundalk. Enlarged in the 1930s by landfill, it was named Harbor Field. The primitive facilities show in this 1937 picture.

The most glamorous event of the decade was the visit of Queen Marie of Roumania on October 20, 1926. Schools were let out to see the pageantry at the War Memorial, but few remember why she came. A bigger show was the campaign speech by Franklin Delano Roosevelt at the Fifth Regiment Armory, October 26, 1932. Few in the audience could have guessed that his election to the presidency a week later was a turning point in world history.

Night Shift—Bethlehem Fairfield Shipbuilding Yard, 1944.

TWO
THE GREAT WAR

With 1939 came the end of innocence as war erupted in Europe and Asia. The United States began arming against contingencies—the Japanese assault on Pearl Harbor in 1941 brought total involvement. After nearly four years of "blood, toil, tears and sweat" in Sir Winston Churchill's great words, the ordeal was over, and we had grown up, nation, city, ourselves.

Baltimore was an important cog in the national war machine. Our specialties were the production line manufacture of ships at the Fairfield Shipbuilding Yard, and elsewhere—383 *Liberty*-type ships, 94 *Victory*-type, 49 big landing craft, and 44 oil tankers. At the Glenn L. Martin plant on Middle River big seaplanes and light bombers were turned out in quantity. Almost everybody was employed in the war effort in some way, whether repairing damaged ships, or making uniforms, C-Rations or radar equipment. Some went off to war as fighting men or merchant seaman, WACS and WAVES and lady Marines, or as doctors, nurses, chaplains and Red Cross aides. All too many never came back. The rest worked long hours at jobs and many volunteered for extra duty on draft boards, civil defense outfits, in the hospitals and at the U.S.O. Because of the shortage of labor, women took over jobs that were traditionally male —driving cabs and street cars, delivering the mail, and working at all sorts of mechanical trades in ship yards and airplane factories. A flood of migrants poured into Baltimore, many of them from the Appalachian region, and the sound of country music became familiar.

There was a job for everyone and plenty of money but not much to do with it. Housing was in short supply, and there just wasn't enough sugar, coffee, meat, shoes or gasoline to meet every desire. A system of rationing was set up with each person getting an allotment of stamps and plastic tokens good for his share of the scarce items. Nylon stockings and cigarettes were hard to find although not actually rationed. Baltimoreans spent a lot of time standing in line to get ration books and stamps, more time to get the goods, rode street cars and buses to work and stayed home on weekends. The shortages and inconveniences were exasperating and there was grumbling about bureaucratic confusion but most of us played the game with good grace. After all, it was little enough trouble compared to the chances of the men on the Murmansk run, the soldiers and marines in the South Pacific jungles or the bomber crews over Germany. People felt like that—it was a sobering experience to live through the great war.

The Fairfield Yard from the air, August 15, 1945 at the peak of production. The war was over but these ships were needed in the post-war relief program.

Launching the S.S. *Maritime Victory* at Fairfield, May 22, 1945. *(below)* Maiden flight of the Glenn L. Martin *Mars* out of Middle River, July 3, 1942. Largest class of sea planes ever built, they ferried troops and supplies in the Pacific theatre of war.

The first Baltimoreans officially involved in the war were in the Fifth Regiment of the Maryland National Guard which was mustered into Federal service ten months before Pearl Harbor. *(below)* Afterwards, the Armory was the collecting point for those drafted into the Army. These were among the last in March, 1945.

Merchant marine training ships at Pier 2, Pratt Street, 1944.

Home cooking on shore leave—New Year's dinner, 1945.

After work in Beulah Hardiman's bar, 1943.

The ship builders at Fairfield.

Building bombers at the Glenn L. Martin plant, 1943.
(below) Migrant war workers—they did their part.

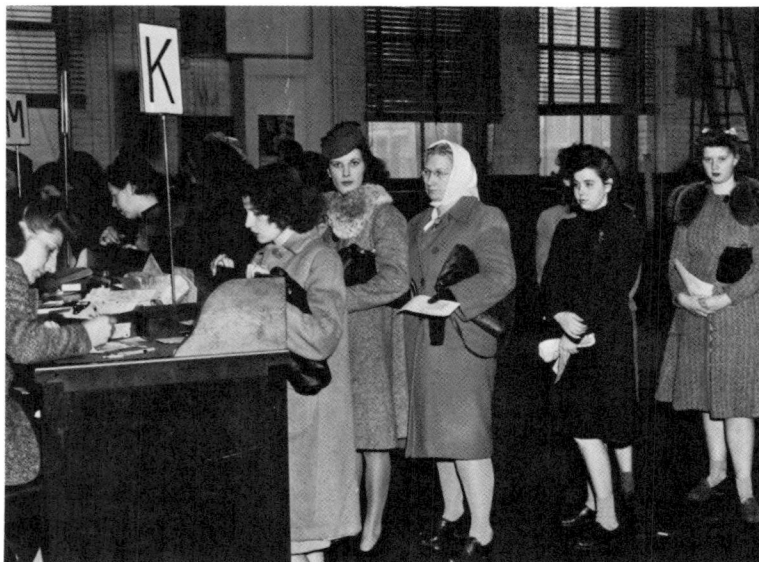

Rationing memories, 1945—
books, permits, stamps, tokens.

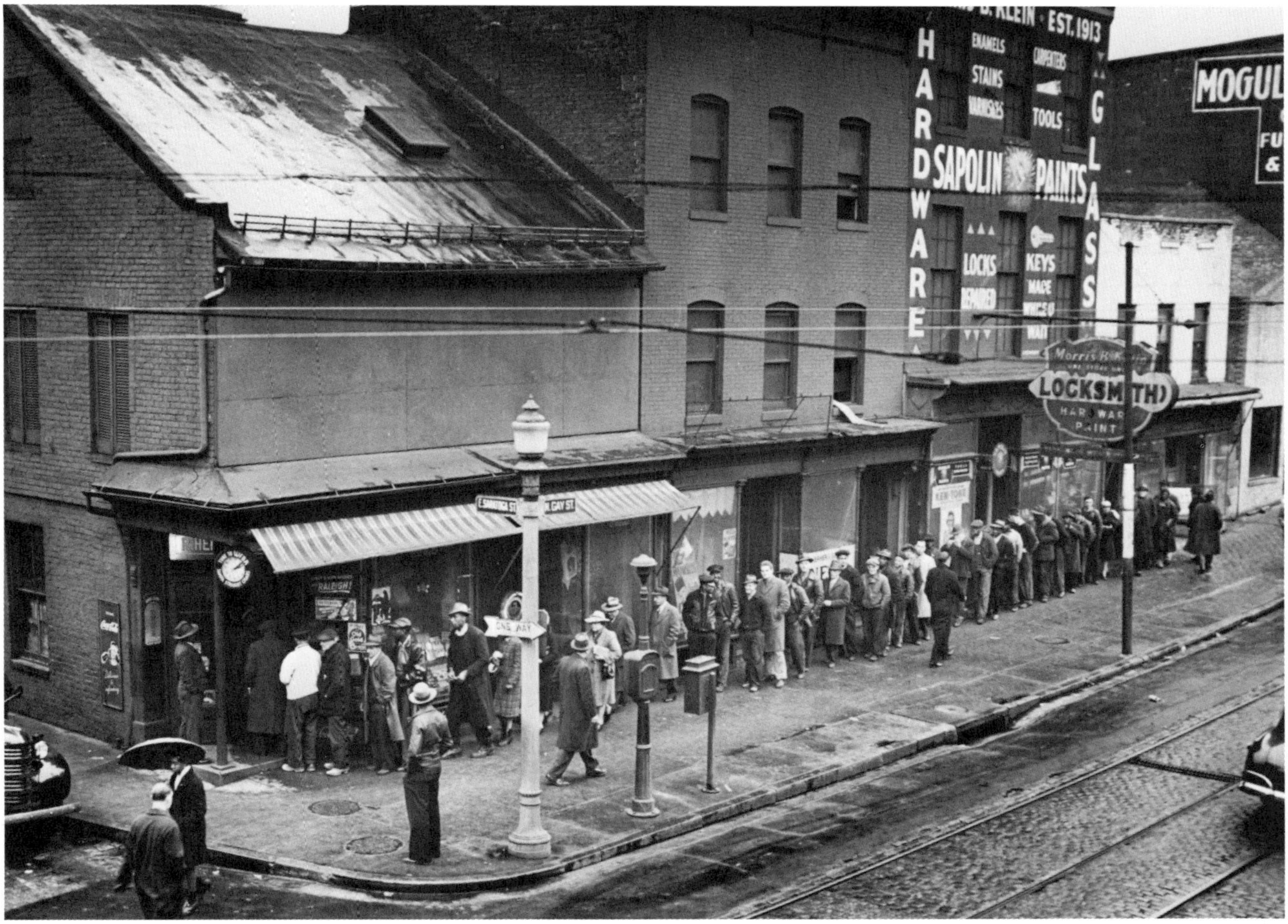

Waiting for cigarettes (Gay and Saratoga Street) and for nylon stockings (Lexington and Liberty Streets), 1945.

VE Day, May 7, 1945 at Howard and Lexington Streets —the European war was over. *(below)* First soldiers released from service, May 12, 1945.

It's all over now—VJ Day, August 14, 1945. Everybody was at Charles and Baltimore Streets that night.

THREE
THE BIG SCENE

The port had always been the key element in the city's character, and after the war it began to change rapidly. Motor trucks took over the transport of fish and produce throughout the Bay region and the sailing bugeyes and skipjacks no longer came to Baltimore. For the same reason Bay steam boat service dwindled and ended in 1963 when the line to Norfolk was discontinued. The port's business was increasingly concerned with bulk cargo—coal and wheat, iron and copper ore, crude oil and phosphate rock—which was handled in specialized facilities of the outer harbor. The old "Basin" at Pratt and Light street, Baltimore's original harbor, lost most of its commercial maritime significance but for an occasional banana carrier and a few excursion boats. Big ships seldom came in past Fort McHenry except to the ship repair yards at the east side of Federal Hill.

In 1968 a massive Inner Harbor Urban Renewal Project was launched to replace the old docks and commercial buildings with a yacht marina, new Maryland Academy of Sciences building, office towers and apartment houses. In short, the old harbor will be transformed into a scenic lagoon. The first permanent feature of the new project is the famous U.S. Frigate *Constellation*, built at Fell's Point in 1797.

Harbor Scene, 1945.

Baltimore Harbor at Night, 1949.

LAST OF THEIR KIND

(above) A sailing schooner at Locust Point, 1947, *(below left)* excursion boat *Bay Belle*, 1946. *(below right)* Ferry to Love Point on the Eastern Shore, 1946—nicknamed "Smokey Joe," although on good behavior here.

U.S.S. *George Washington* and *Edmund B. Alexander (above)* at Hawkins Point, German luxury passenger liners seized during World War I and used for troop transports in both wars. The *Washington* burned at this pier, January 16, 1951 and the *Alexander* was scrapped shortly after. *(below)* Sidewheel steamer *F. C. Latrobe*, 1952. Built in Baltimore in 1879, it was one of the port's ice breakers but transported generations of school classes and civic groups on free harbor tours in the warmer months. It was scrapped in the 1960s.

After the war, shipbuilding continued at the Bethlehem Steel Sparrows Point works with larger and larger cargo ships, many of them tankers like *Cities Service Miami* going down the building ways in 1956 *(opposite page)*. Three unusual maritime visitors to Baltimore: *(top)* U.S.S. *Randolph*, a battle-scarred aircraft carrier returning from the Pacific War, October 1945. *(middle)* tanker *Manhattan*, March 1963, displaced over 100,000 tons—it was later famous as the first commercial ship to make the "Northwest Passage" through the Arctic ice pack around Canada to Alaska, *(below)* the world's first nuclear-powered merchant ship, *Savannah*, May 1964.

A nautical scene on Pratt Street, 1954. The Old Bay Line steamer *City of Norfolk* is in the distance. The ship chandler was displaced to Fell's Point by the inner harbor renewal project, and the steamship line ceased operations in 1963.

(above) Shown in 1947 alongside its better known sister, U.S.F. *Constitution,* at Boston, the dismasted *Constellation* looked like a poor bet to survive. *(below)* But by 1969 she was the showpiece of Baltimore's inner harbor project with its restoration well underway, thanks to a devoted band of citizens who refused to admit defeat in spite of all manner of discouragement. Today the ship and the project are much closer to completion than this picture shows.

Both the electric trolley car and the steam locomotive were obsolete by 1963, but their fascination lingers on. *(left above)* Does anyone remember the "old" Colts of 1948? *(left below)* A Western Maryland Railroad heavy freight engine. *(right)* South from the 29th Street Bridge, 1946.

Swampy Harbor Field was superseded in 1950 by Friendship International Airport in Anne Arundel County. It was so spacious that it adapted easily to the change from the propeller planes of the 50s to the huge jets of the 60s.

THE STREET SCENE

The character of the post-war city felt the standardizing pressures of the automobile, big business and nationally advertised brands, but some of Baltimore's individuality survived—at least for a time. Bodine caught a good deal of the flavor of this passing scene in his photographs of the odd details of the cityscape which make it interesting.

Some things have gone forever, like the old Lexington Market, the biggest of the public markets, with two blocks under roof, flanked by dozens of canopied street stalls. On the other hand, the street hucksters, called "Ay-Rabs" in Baltimore still prowl the streets of the inner city with rented wagons and carts peddling soft crabs, fish, fruits and vegetables in season. This is the last commercial use of the horse—except for racetracks.

The Baltimore street scene is played against a backdrop of buildings—in the old neighborhoods the classic textures are weathered wood, painted brick, white marble, and cast iron—but the variety is astonishing.

This Lexington Market burned down March 25, 1949, and was replaced by a two-block modern building—but the street stalls are no more.

Cabbages, bananas, chickens and fish—and service with a smile.

FACES AND FACADES

(left) West Mulberry Street.
(right above) Restaurant in the shadow of the Guilford Avenue viaduct, 1947, and its proprietors, Martin J. Welsh and his sons.
(left below) Bodine titled it "Tough kids."
(right below) We have no title for this 1956 picture near Hollins Market.

MORE FACES AND FACADES

(left) On "Antiques Row," North Howard Street, about 1948.
(below) Fell's Point Barber Shop, 1636 Thames Street, 1956

Founded on North Howard Street in 1876 by Jacob Smith, this treasure trove of 150,000 books was the bibliophile's delight—but went out of business in 1965.

Fire insurance underwriters would consider this wooden house at High and Low Streets an impossible risk, but it survived 150 years only to be demolished for an urban renewal project about 1950.
(right above) Every American actor and actress of importance played John T. Ford's Grand-Opera House on Fayette Street near Eutaw from 1871 until it was demolished in 1964.
(right below) The Sunpapers Building is on the site of the 1850 Calvert Station, once the commuters' destination from Mt. Washington, Ruxton and Parkton.

Baltimore's first gas street lamp was lighted in 1817, the last one put out in 1957.
(above) Willy Hoffman, lamplighter, demonstrates his craft, 1947.
(below) Tyson Street residents made the city keep the old cast iron lamp standards, although converted to electricity.
(right) New Deal Barber Shop, 1951.

ROWHOUSE CITY

In the 19th century Baltimore's rapid population growth was accommodated by group housing, row after row and block after block of individual residences, not tenements or apartments as in New York. There was a lot more variety than outsiders think, and the scale was human-size.
(above) Central Avenue, since demolished.
(right) Shakespeare Street on Fell's Point.

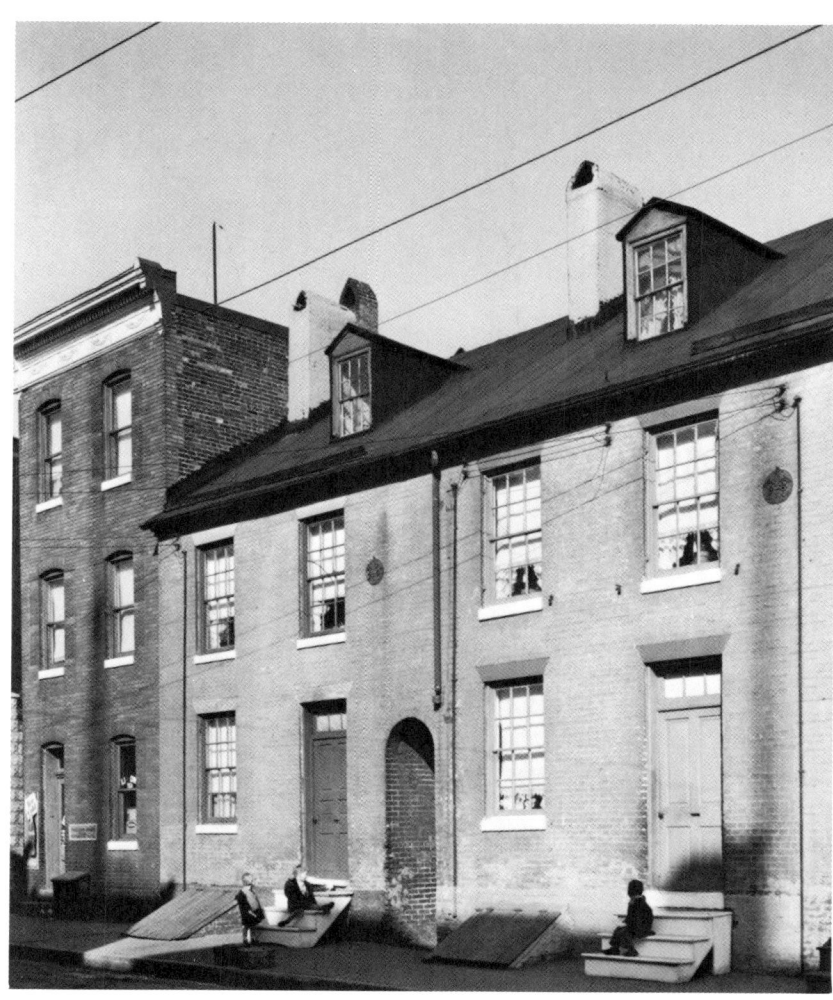

The cock-eyed block—100 West Montgomery Street, 1948. How did this happen?

STREET PATTERNS

(left above) Marble steps and yellow brick, Penrose Avenue and Pulaski Street. Bodine used this negative for one of his most famous pictures. Cropped tightly around the step area and turned sideways, he made his prize winning "Cubist Design" of 1947.
(below) Decorator's triumph: scenic screens, grained woodwork, painted brick, 1946.
(above) Neatness counts—tipping the steps up at night saves paint. Fountain Street in Fell's Point, 1947.

ALLEY PATTERNS

Back yards and alleys were often more interesting than the street fronts. Decorative cast iron railing was a Baltimore manufacturing specialty a century ago, exported to New Orleans and San Francisco. Unfortunately, less and less of it survives in its native city.

THE PLAYERS

Jones, the Howard Street costumer, *(above)* could fit you out for a stage play, an opera, or a fancy dress ball, but the roles we play in the work-a-day drama and our costumes outdo fiction. Bodine had a flair for dramatizing common-place occupations. He especially admired the grace and simple dignity of craftsmen whose traditional skills are rapidly being displaced by impersonal machinery. These pictures record some of the supporting players who gave style and character to Baltimore's pageant of the past four decades.

Baltimore is largely built of brick—houses, office buildings and churches. Brickmaking is our oldest industry. This 1935 picture shows the kilns in Westport where bricks were fired for two centuries or more. In 1828 over one million local bricks were used in the Shot Tower—a truly monumental exhibit of brick masonry.
(below) In 1936 when this was taken Baltimore was the U. S. straw hat manufacturing capital and no gentleman's summer wardrobe was complete without a straw "boater" or "skimmer," as they were sometimes called.

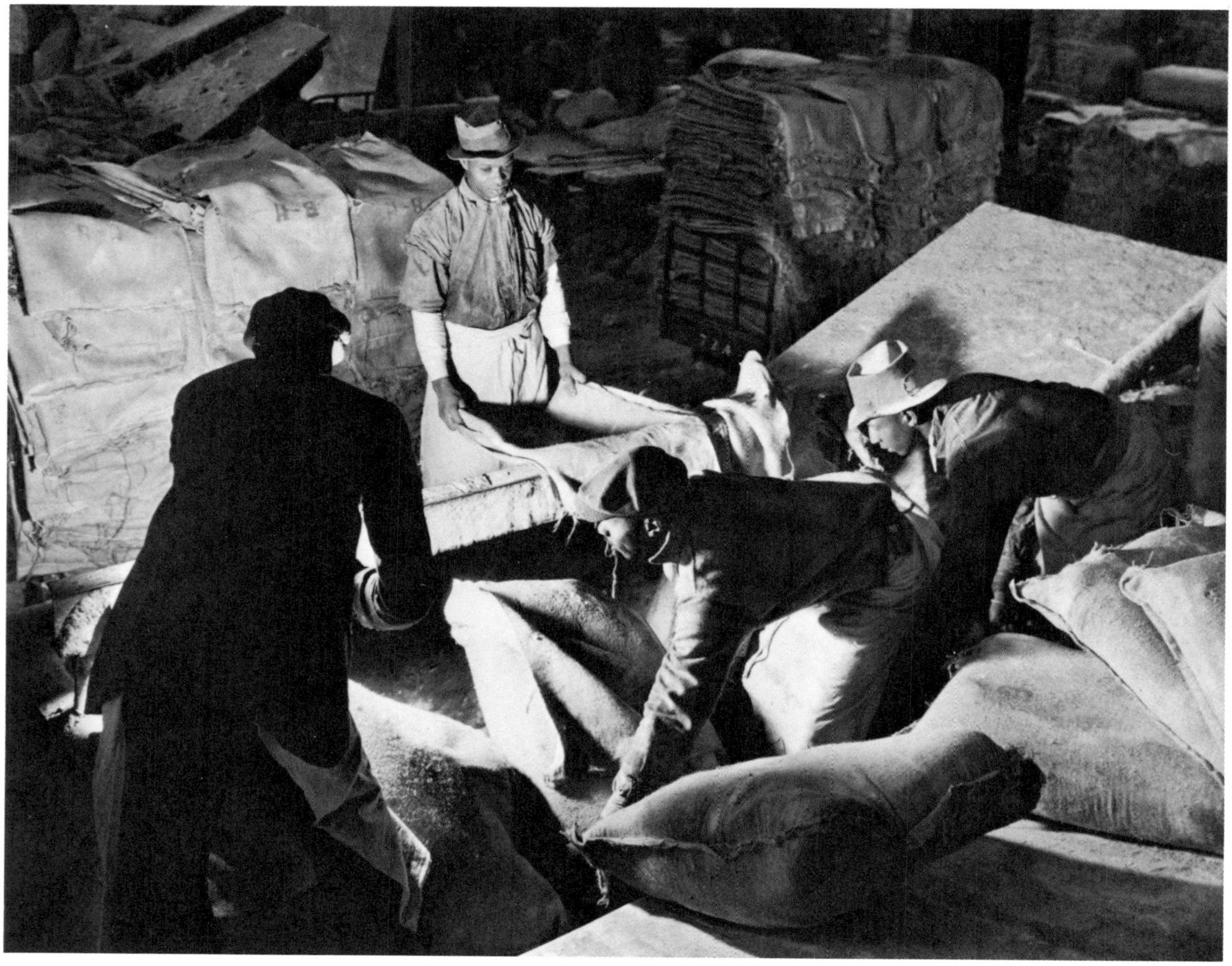

Bagging sugar, 1933.

Longshoremen, 1968.

INDUSTRIAL ENSEMBLES

Tugboat pilot.

Welder.

HARBOR FACES, 1954

Rigger.

CRAFTSMEN

Oyster shucker at Dunlop's on Howard Street.
Peggy, auto mechanic.
Belle, machinist.

Bill Schmidt, blacksmith.
Charlie, itinerant knife sharpener, 1962.
Violin maker at Hildebrandt's.
H. A. Smith, locksmith, 1948.

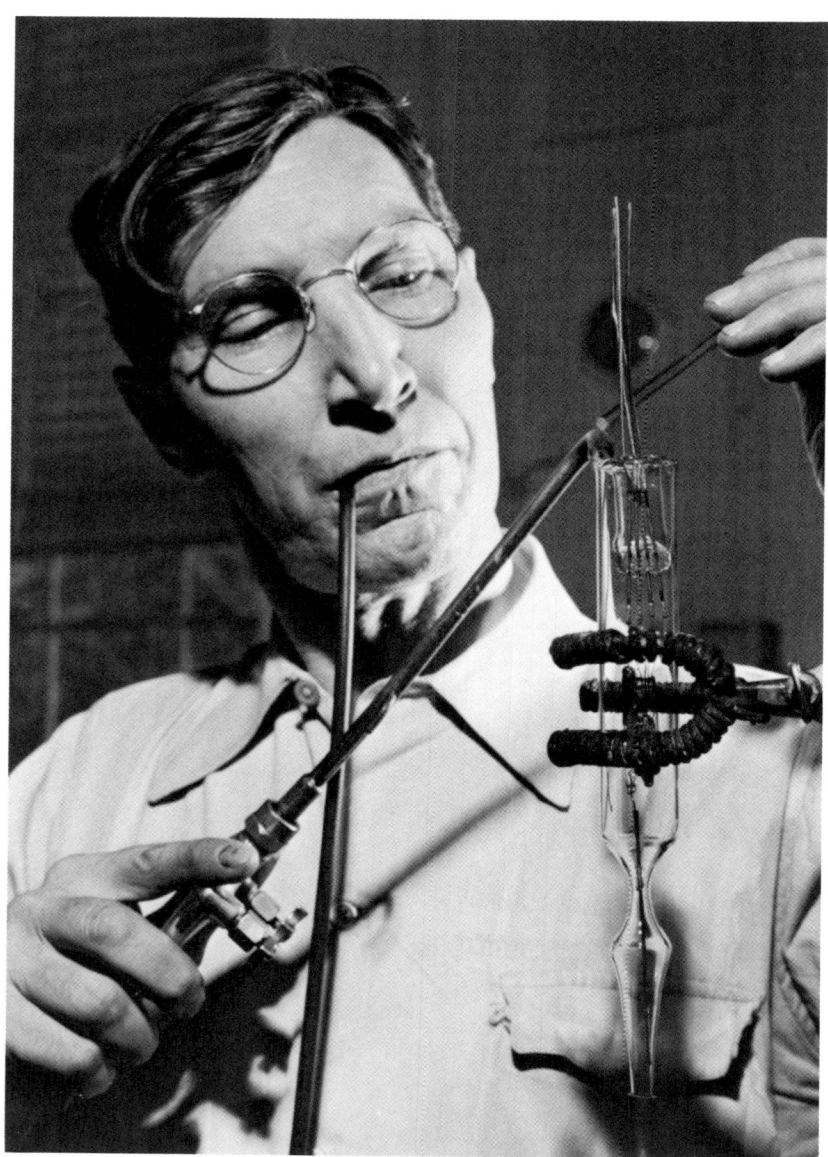

SPECIALISTS

Glassblowing is an art.
(above) John H. Lehman making intricate scientific devices at Johns Hopkins, 1959.
(below) Nelson Hume making perfume bottles, 1955.

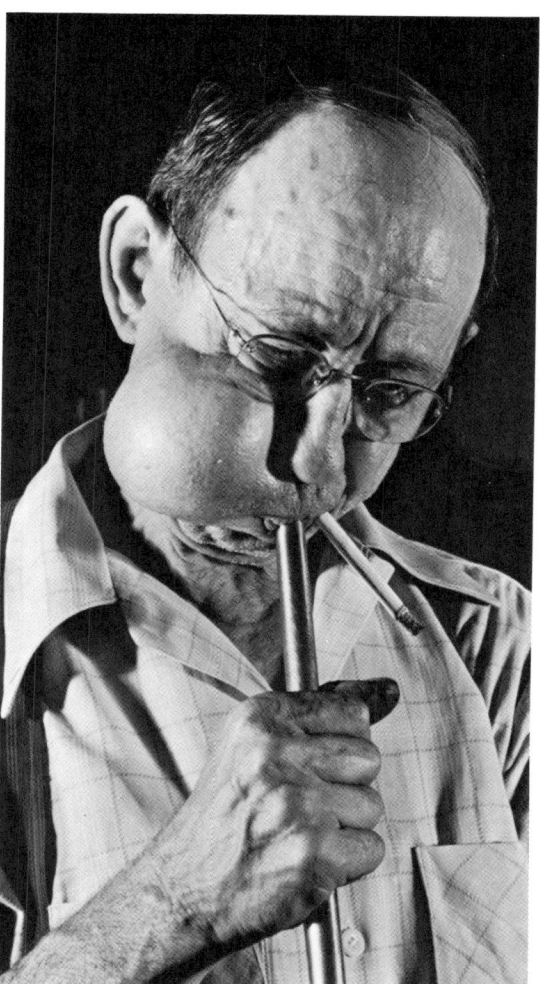

Skin specialist, Baltimore Street, 1944.

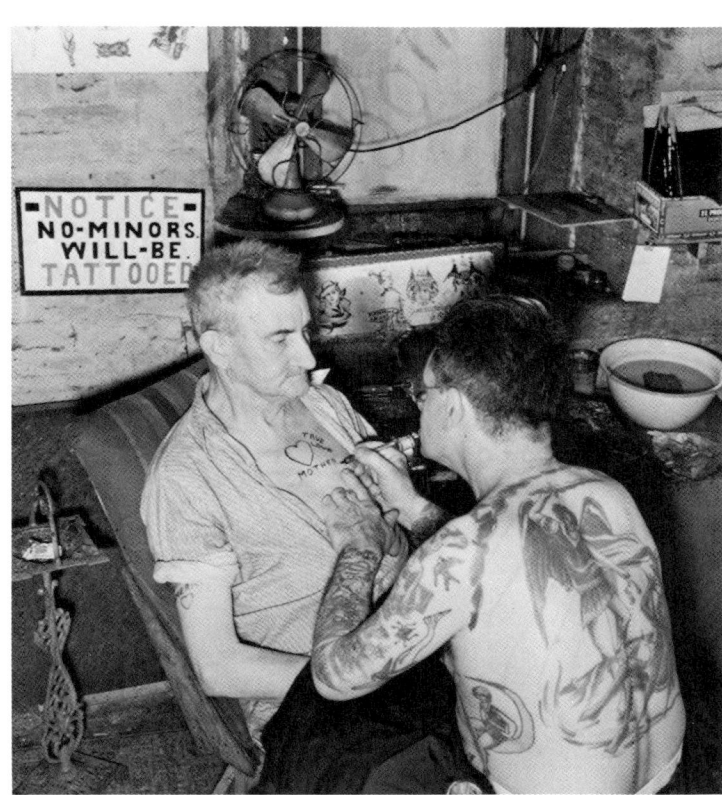

J. Alvin H. Ruperti, bookbinder, 1932.

Oil fire, Key Highway.

Hosing down a cobblestone street, 1951.

PUBLIC PROTECTORS

(left) Through snow and slush, 1935.

FOR THE INTERMISSION

(above) Preparing Diamondback Terrapin for stew at the Maryland Club, 1957.
Harley Brinsfield launches a sub on McMechen Street, 1948.

(above) Haussner's, the picturesque restaurant, 1949.
(below) Mint Julep in the Belvedere Bar.

(right) Dr. and Mrs. Chao Ming Chen, importers of oriental art. Their home on 29th Street was a museum for connoisseurs of Asian *objets d'art.*

FEATURED PLAYERS

Whether by choice or accident, some people play their part in the spotlight. Bodine had the opportunity of photographing a good many of the leading public personalities of the past forty years both formally posed and in action.

They are often very penetrating commentaries, perhaps more so than either Bodine or the subject expected. A great deal could be written about these featured players of the Baltimore pageant, but the pictures are intended to tell the story here—with a little assistance from the captions.

(above) Monsieur Louis Crest's French Bakery, North Howard Street, 1944.
(middle) Greenberg's Bakery, Lexington Street.
(below) William J. Wiseman, grocer, East Eager Street.

BALTIMORE POLITICIANS

(top) Daniel J. Loden, sometime City Collector of License Fees and Rents, and one of "the good old b'hoys" in ward politics, 1928.
(middle) Marie Bauernschmidt, long-time head of the Public School Association, reformer and political gadfly, 1946.
(below) City Councilman Dominic Mimi Di Pietro and constituents, 1967.

(top) A political chore—Mayor Howard W. Jackson eating oysters, 1938.

(top right) Baltimore-born Governor and Mrs. Spiro T. Agnew, 1967—two years later, Vice-President.

(below) Mayor Thomas D'Alesandro, Jr., and family, 1947. The tallest boy, "young Tommy," became Mayor twenty years later.

(top) Mayor Jackson at his City Hall desk, 1938.
(middle) Another Baltimore boy, Governor Herbert R. O'Conor, addressing the legislature, 1940.
(below) Governor Theodore R. McKeldin afloat at Annapolis, 1948—previously Mayor (1943-47) and subsequently Mayor (1963-67).
(bottom) City Council President Thomas J. D'Alesandro, III, (Mayor 1967-71) and City Comptroller Hyman Pressman at the Board of Estimates, 1966.

BALTIMORE CIVIC FORCES

(top left) Rev. Philip Berrigan, S.S.J., slum fighter, 1965.
(right) Rev. Dr. Don Frank Fenn, champion of liberal causes and chairman of the Housing Authority of Baltimore, 1947-50.
(above) Esther Lazarus, Director of the Baltimore Department of Welfare, 1945-1960.
(bottom) Rev. Fred J. Hanna, inner city social ministry in the 1960's.

Glenn L. Martin (1886-1955), pioneer aviator, aircraft designer and manufacturer on Middle River, creator of the *Clipper*, the *Mars*, and the famous World War II B 26 *Marauder* bomber. *(bottom)* Jacob Blaustein, (1892-1970) oil business pioneer, unofficial adviser to five presidents, delegate to the U. N. General Assembly, and philanthropist, 1960.

CELEBRITIES

(top) Dorothy Lamour, actress and cosmetic manufacturer at Rockland Mill, Falls Road, and her husband, William Howard, 1963.

(middle) The Duke and Duchess of Windsor at Blakeford, 1959, with A. Aubrey Bodine and reporter Audrey Bishop.

(bottom) Elizabeth "Toots" Barger, national champion duckpin bowler, 1947 and after.

Henry Louis Mencken, (1880-1956) journalist, writer, iconoclast, wit, conversationalist, linguist and enthusiastic amateur musician. By birth and afterwards by choice a Baltimorean, he was a hero to Aubrey Bodine and many of that generation.
(below) with his wife, Sara Haardt, 1933.
(above) with his brother August, 1955, in the back yard of 1524 Hollins Street—he chopped the fire wood, too.

(above) John Dos Passos, (1886-1970), novelist, historian, working in the Peabody Institute Library, 1960.
(middle) Louis Cheslock, composer, musician, instructor at the Peabody Institute, 1964.
(below right) Gerald White Johnson, journalist, historian, 1950.

FRIENDS OF MENCKEN

(above) Kate Coplan, display genius for the library, 1963.
(below) Adelyn Dohme Breeskin, Director of the Baltimore Museum of Art, 1942-62.

OF THE ARTS

(above) Stanislav Rembski, portraitist.
(middle) Perna Krick, painter, sculptor. Reuben Kramer, sculptor.
(below) Grace H. Turnbull, painter, sculptor, Greek scholar, poet, and philanthropist.

MUSICIANS

(above) Bob Iula and his popular dance band, 1930.
(below left) A famous prima donna of the Metropolitan Opera, Rosa Ponselle, retired to Baltimore and a whirlwind of activity in auditioning and coaching students, 1959.
(below right) Baltimore Symphony strings.

JOURNALISTS

(above) Frank Richardson Kent, (1877-1958) editor and commentator for the *Sun* from 1900 to 1950. His column, "The Great Game of Politics" sharply criticized politicos and parties, especially Democrats.

(below) Richard Q. Yardley, cartoonist, joined the *Sunpapers* the same year as Bodine, and they were great friends. His humorous drawings were as much a part of the Baltimore scene as Bodine's photographs.

On the lawn of Forest Park High School about 1935.

SCHOLARS AND THEIR SCHOOLS

A large part of our lives is spent in school. For some this means twenty-five years from grade school through dancing school, high school, college and post-graduate university work. In Baltimore the highest aspirations are symbolized by The Johns Hopkins University, the great gift, almost a century ago, of a businessman who was what we now call a school drop-out. Be that as it may, Johns Hopkins brought more fame to the city than any other man.

But higher education began much earlier than Hopkins. The medical school of the University of Maryland was founded in 1812, and flourishes today. Business and philanthropy combined to establish the Maryland Institute for the Promotion of Mechanic Arts in 1848 which still goes strongly today, although the emphasis is on the fine arts. And in 1887 Dr. John Franklin Goucher began "The Woman's College of Baltimore" which now bears his name.

No catalog of local educational institutions is intended here—this is Bodine's sample.

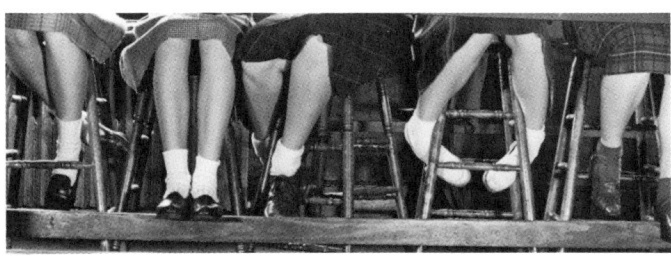

SCHOOL DAYS

SCHOOL DAYS

February at Homewood, 1964

The first president of The Johns Hopkins University in 1876 was Daniel Coit Gilman. This quadrangle and the towered hall on the Homewood campus are named after him. Dr. Milton Stover Eisenhower, president 1956-1967 and 1971 was the last one Bodine photographed.

HOPKINS SCIENTISTS

(above) Dr. Robert Williams Wood (1868-1955), professor of physics from 1901, specialized in the theory of light and optics. Also a poet and science fictioneer, he wrote *How to Tell the Birds from the Flowers*, illustrated with his own drawings.

(below) Dr. Elmer Verner McCollum (1879-1967), professor of biochemistry from 1917, was the discoverer of vitamins A and D.

HOPKINS HUMANISTS

(above left) Dr. William Foxwell Albright, (1891-1971), professor of Semitic languages, and a great archeologist, wrote the influential *From Stone Age to Christianity*.
(above right) Dr. Arthur O. Lovejoy, (1873-1962), professor of philosophy, is famous for *The Great Chain of Being*.
(below) Simone Brangier Boas, sculptor and gourmet cook, and her husband, Dr. George Boas, professor of philosophy, 1957. Lovejoy said, "George is the only philosopher I know who served in both the Army (World War I) and Navy (World War II) and who knows how to milk a cow."

Johns Hopkins provided for a hospital along with a School of Medicine in his great bequest. The dome of the administration building on Broadway is better known around the nation and the world than any other Baltimore landmark because of the countless visiting patients and students who sought help and knowledge here.

(above) Dr. William Henry Welch, (1850-1935), on the right, with Dr. Karl Sudhoff of Germany, October 1929. Called "our greatest statesman in the field of public health" by President Hoover, and the "dean of American Medicine" by many, Dr. Welch was known affectionately to students as "Popsy." Sudhoff founded the Institute of Medical History at Leipsig, and came here to help inaugurate the Welch Medical Library and the Hopkins Department of History of Medicine.
(middle) Max Broedel, (1870-1941) artist, organized the Department of Art as applied to medicine. His medical illustrations are classics; his personality inimitable.
(below) Dr. Thomas S. Cullen, (1868-1953) longtime professor of gynecology.

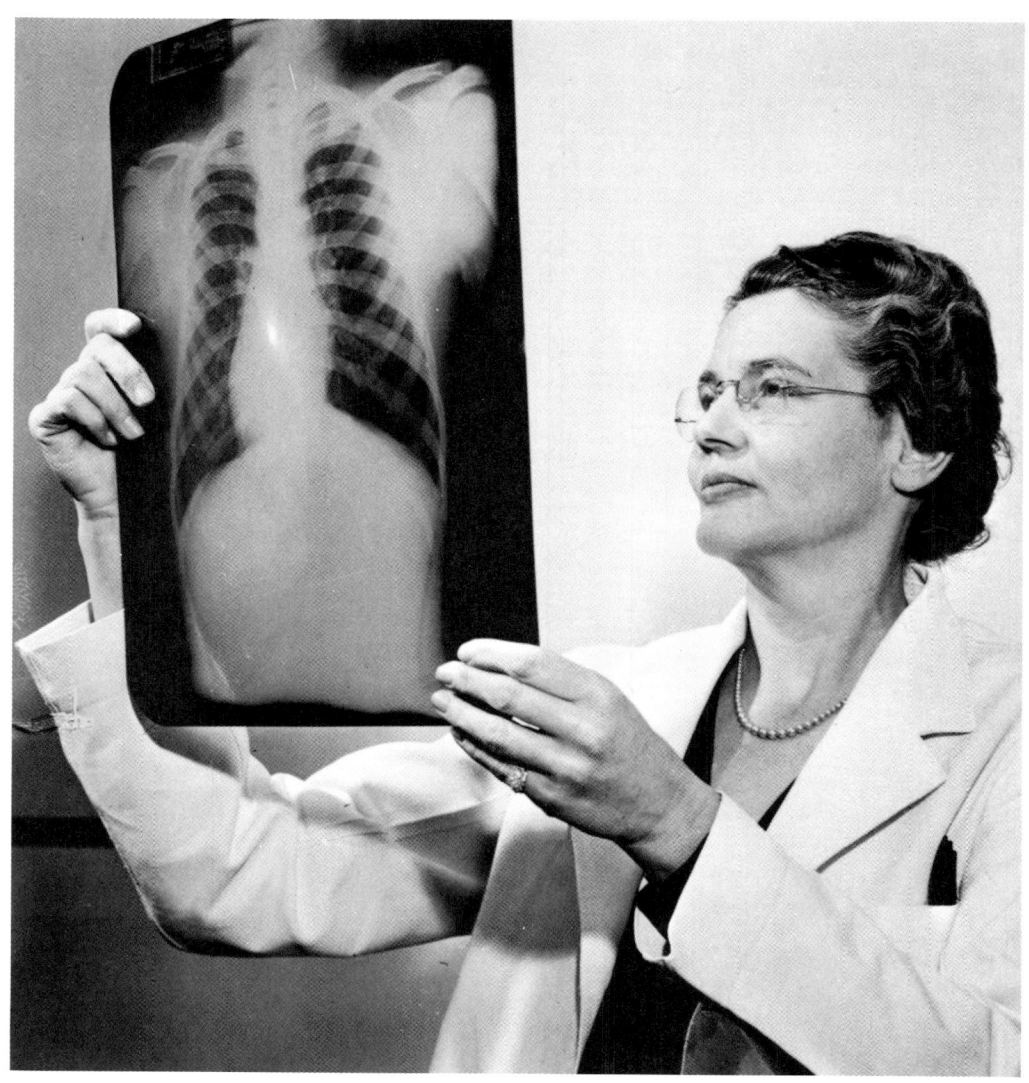

(top) Dr. Helen Brooke Taussig, pediatrician, specialized in rheumatic fever and heart malformation. She formulated the theory for corrective surgery on what are called "Blue Babies," which her surgical colleague, Dr. Alfred Blalock, successfully performed for the first time in 1944.
(below left) Proved first on this dog, the Taussig-Blalock heart operation cured these two "Blue Babies" in 1950. Both doctors were Hopkins graduates.

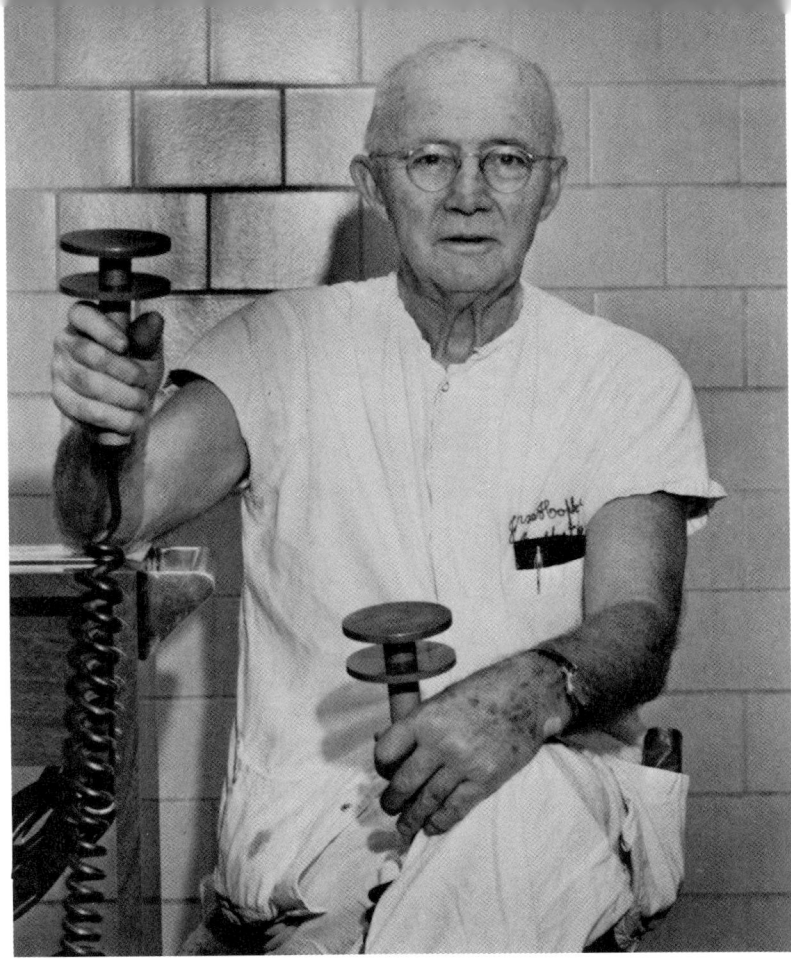

(above) Dr. William Bennett Kouwenhoven, professor of electrical engineering, developed the electric shock technique for emergency treatment of heart failure.

(below) Dr. W. Horsley Gantt worked with the great scientist, Ivan P. Pavlov, in Leningrad in the 1920's, and continued his researches in the interaction of psychology and physiology at Johns Hopkins ever since.

Vignettes of Johns Hopkins Hospital, 1964:
(1) Case discussion in Turner Auditorium.
(2) Making the rounds with Dr. Louis Lasagna.
(3) Coffee break.
(4) Psychological evaluation through art.
(5) Nurse's station with students.

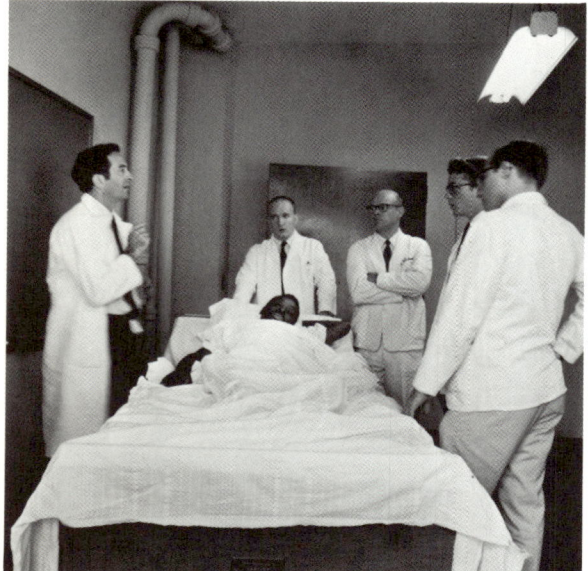

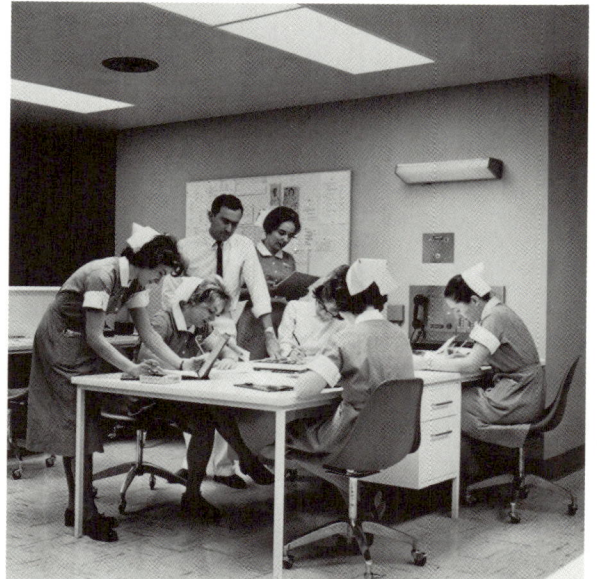

(top) All together, wider please! University of Maryland Dental School, 1937.
(middle) Davidge Hall, 1956. Built in 1812 it is one of the oldest medical school buildings in the nation.
(bottom) Lecture room in Davidge Hall, with objects of interest to medical students.

GOUCHER
COLLEGE

(left) The first campus was in the neighborhood of the Lovely Lane Methodist Church (upper picture). Dr. John Franklin Goucher was minister, church builder, and college founder. The building beyond the lamp post was Goucher Hall, whose portico is silhouetted below.
Left below is the Library reading room in Glitner Hall.
(below) The College Center and Kraushaar Auditorium on the present Towson campus.

(above) Morning break at the Maryland Institute on Mount Royal Avenue, 1935.
(left) Back to work.

Strange metamorphosis! In 1965 the Institute acquired the Mount Royal Railroad Station and transformed it in the name of art. The art had changed, too.

FESTIVALS

Begun in 1911 by the Women's Civic League, the annual Flower Mart in early May around the base of the Washington Monument was the city's largest folk festival for sixty years. Streets were roped off and booths set up where garden clubs and other civic groups sold potted plants, cut flowers, candy and cakes and a specialty, whole lemons with a stick of peppermint candy inserted as a straw. In recent years there were amusement rides for the kiddies, crab cakes sold in vast quantities, art exhibitions, and more and more of everything—especially people. Paradoxically, as downtown became less residential more people hungered for what had once been a neighborhood fête and the crush became unmanageable. Its purposes outgrown, the Mart was discontinued in 1971.

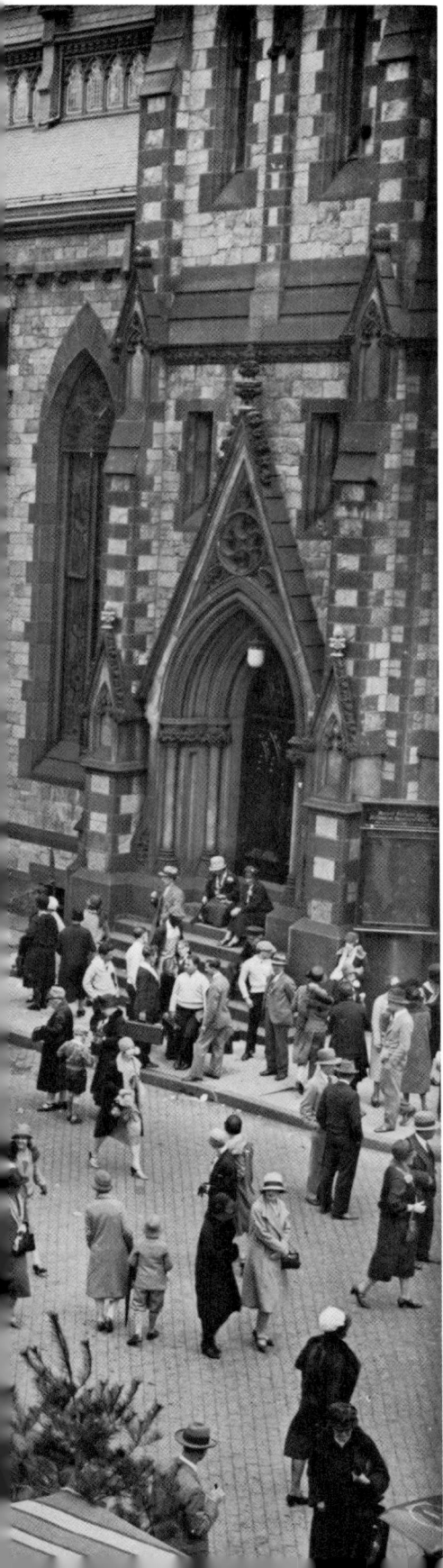

Other Festivals
(1) Easter egg hunt, Patterson Park.
(2) Bolton Street Fair, May 1956.
(3) and (4) The counter culture's Read Street Festival, 1970.

(above) The circus comes to town—elephant parade, 1956.
(right) "Betsy," the artistic chimpanzee, with Arthur Watson, Director of the Baltimore Zoo, 1953. She could finger paint as well as any two year-old, and her pictures sold briskly at $25 each for the Zoo's benefit.

THE SPORT OF KINGS

Once thought of as the sport of royalty, horse racing today is a democratic device for collecting taxes from the betting public. Still, the noble qualities remain: the beautiful animals, the color and the excitement. The century-old track of the Maryland Jockey Club at Pimlico is not only a local institution of importance, but better known to a good many outsiders than the Washington Monument. The Preakness Race in mid-May ranks with the Kentucky Derby and the Belmont Stakes as a champion test for three year-olds. It was a proud day for

Baltimore when Native Dancer, Maryland raised and owned, won the Preakness in 1953. *(below)* Clubhouse turn, 1948. Ninety-six years old, the picturesque Victorian Club House burned down in 1966.

(above) Coming into the stretch.
(next) Waiting.
(below) Down to the wire—
Preakness, 1948.

Native Dancer, "The Gray Ghost," won 21 out of 22 starts, including the 1953 Preakness and $785,000, and retired to a life of indolence and pleasure at Sagamore Farms in the Worthington Valley until he died in 1967.

Fairground races were usually taken in as part of a family excursion which included the 4-H exhibits, hot dogs, and the Ferris wheel.
(above) Bel Air Fair trotters, 1932.
(left) Timonium State Fair, 1956.
(bottom) Auto racing at the Bel Air Fair, 1930's.

The annual Maryland Hunt Cup raced over fences on several farms in the Green Spring Valley is both more social and amateur than Pimlico. The single race takes a few minutes; the spectators enjoy a day-long party.
(above) Billy Barton, Maryland's greatest jumper, won all the major hunt races and in 1928 almost took the English Grand National Steeplechase. *(below)* Maryland Hunt Cup, 1949.

SPORTS FOR EVERYONE

One of the advantages Baltimore enjoys over larger cities is the nearness of open country and the broad Chesapeake Bay. With horse, dog and gun, row boat, line and crab net we can hunt bird, beast and fish within an hour's drive and with a good chance of success.

Some look upon fox hunting as the King of Sports. On Thanksgiving Day hundreds of spectators visit St. John's Church in Worthington Valley to witness the traditional blessing of the hounds of the Green Spring Valley Hunt Club. Others prefer the company of a pair of English setters in the pursuit of the elusive quail. *(right)* Duck hunting was even more popular, especially on the Susquehanna Flats where until 1940 the sink box rig shown below was permitted. The hunters sat right in the midst of their string of decoys a hundred yards offshore. It was cold and wet but a very effective technique.

(above) A boat, a net, some string and a few fish heads are all you need to catch the Chesapeake Bay Blue Crab—the gourmet's delight and the fisherman's best bet.

(right) Motorcycling is a good deal noisier than crabbing, but it has its devotees in the Baltimore area.

Although some winters there is very little ice in Baltimore, skating is popular when possible. *(above)* Crack-the-whip, 1929. *(middle)* Little league ice hockey on the Homeland ponds. *(bottom)* The artificial ice rink at Memorial Stadium, 1959.

Baltimore's amateur sports run the gamut. Badminton has a small but enthusiastic following *(top)*. *(bottom)* Jousting was adopted as the official state sport, but if any sport deserved this title it is the old Indian game of lacrosse. *(right, above)*. Teams from Johns Hopkins, the Naval Academy and the University of Maryland usually dominate the national rankings, while the wholly amateur Mt. Washington Lacrosse Club beats all of them. Soccer is popular in East Baltimore *(bottom)* and the area produces some good teams.

The first big Baltimore stadium of 1921 was little more than an earthen bowl with plank seats, but the U. S. Naval Academy played some important football games there.
(left) In 1954 on the same site a new War Memorial Stadium was built, and Baltimore entered the major leagues with the football Colts and baseball Orioles, both of which have won national championships several times.
(above) The All Star Game, 1958, and a full house.

THE NEW BALTIMORE

The signs were there in the 1950's—the urban core was losing its old character as the automobile dispersed the population and carried retail business to suburban shopping centers. Was there any way to cope with downtown decline? A remarkable combination of business and financial leaders prepared a plan in 1958. It proposed no less than the demolition of 33 acres in the heart of the city and the creation of a new complex of business, government, recreational and residential buildings with copious parking facilities underground, spacious park areas, and a controlled development program. Scouted by many as an impossible dream, it was adopted by Mayor Thomas D'Alesandro, Jr., as the Charles Center Urban Renewal Project. A retired businessman, Jay Jefferson Miller, agreed to serve as chairman of the project at the remarkable salary of one dollar a year—after a dozen dollars to Jeff Miller and millions more from public and private investors, it was completed on time and as promised.

A glimpse of the future, it was also an end to A. Aubrey Bodine's Baltimore. Some of his last pictures show the activities in the new plazas of Charles Center which now became the favorite locations for art festivals, public occasions, and even a City Fair.

Hopkins Place and statue of Gen. John Mifflin Hood before Charles Center was begun.

Sun Building, Charles and Baltimore Streets, built in 1905, demolished 1964. Bodine worked here for thirty years. It is now the site of the Morris Mechanic Theatre.

Where the Charles Center demolition started in 1958
(top) Charles and Fayette Streets, 1941.
(bottom) Lexington Street at Charles, 1941.

(right) Jay Jefferson Miller, 1964, mainspring of the Charles Center project, in front of the first of the new buildings, aptly named #1 Charles Center.
(below) Center Plaza, 1970. #1 Charles Center at right.

Charles Center almost completed, June 21, 1970.

141

At the first Greater Baltimore Arts Festival in the new Hopkins Plaza, about where General Hood once stood, May 1968.

The new Street Scene in
Charles Center.

Looking west from new Post Office site, 1969

From Federal Hill, November 15, 1967.

The shape of things to come?
Jones Falls Expressway, 1963.

Drilling at Fort McHenry, 1968

INDEX

Agnew, Spiro T. 93
Airplanes 36, 37, 41, 60
Akron, U.S.N. 36
Albright, Dr. William F. 109
Antiques Row 66
Arts Festival, Greater Baltimore 142
Badminton 134
Bagging Sugar 80
Baltimore Harbor at Night 50
Baltimore Street 20, 49, 138
Banana Boat 8
Barger, Elizabeth 97
Baseball 136
Bauernschmidt, Marie 92
Bay Belle 52
Beaver Dam quarries 29
Belair Fair 128
Belvedere Bar 89
Berrigan, Rev. Philip 95
Bethlehem Fairfield shipyard 39, 40, 41, 44
Bethlehem Sparrows Point shipyard 54
Betsy 123
Betterton 30
Billy Barton 129
Bishop, Audrey 97
Blaustein, Jacob 96
Blue Babies 112
Boats vii, 4, 6-8, 30, 34, 39-41, 43, 50-57
Boas, Dr. and Mrs. George 109
Bodine, A. Aubrey 97
Bolton Street Fair 122
Breeskin, Adelyn D. 100
Brick Maker 79
Brinsfield, Harley 88
Broadway 13
Broedel, Max 111
Calvert Station 69
Canton 10
Carlin's Park 28

Cathedral, Palm Sunday snow 1
Cathedral Street 25
Central Avenue 72
Charles Center 137-143
Charles Street 49, 138, 139
Chen, Chao Ming 91
Cheslock, Louis 99
Circus Parade 123
Cities Service Miami, S.S. 54
City of Norfolk, S.S. 56
City Hall 24
Clifton Park 29
Cobblestones 87
Constellation, U.S.F. 57
Constitution, U.S.F. vii, 57
Coplan, Kate 100
Crest, Louis 90
Cubist Design 74
Cullen, Dr. Thomas S. 111
Curtiss-Wright Airport 37
D'Alesandro, Thomas, Jr. 93
D'Alesandro, Thomas J., III 93, 94
Davidge Hall 115
Dickeyville 18
Di Pietro, Dominic M. 92
Dos Passos, John 99
Downtown, looking west 146
Druid Hill Park 3, 26, 27
Edmund B. Alexander, S.S. 53
Eisenhower, Dr. Milton S. 107
Enoch Pratt Free Library 25, 100
Exeter Street 17
Fayette Street iii, 69, 139
Federal Hill, view from ix, 146
Fell's Point 66, 75
Fell's Point Barber Shop 66
Fenn, Rev. Don Frank 95
Fifth Regiment Armory 38, 42
Fire Boat Torrent 34
Fires 35, 87

Fishing x, 30, 132
Flower Mart 120, 121
Ford's Theatre 69
Forest Park High School 104
Fort McHenry 148
Fountain Street 75
Fox hunting 130
Franklin Square 15
French Bakery 90
Friends of Art 22
Friendship International Airport 60
Gantt, Dr. W. H. 113
Gas lamps 70
Gay Street 47
George Washington, S.S. 53
Goucher College 116-117
Green Spring Valley Hunt Club 130
Greenberg's Bakery 90
Gudgeon Fishing x, 30
Guilford Avenue 24, 65
Hanna, Rev. Fred J. 95
Harbor ix, 4, 6-10, 43, 50-53, 55-57, 80, 81
Harbor Field 37
Harbor Scene 51
Hardiman, Beulah 44
Haussner's Restaurant 89
Hawkins Point 53
High and Low Streets 68
Hokey Cart 14
Hollins Street 12
Homeland lakes 133
Hood, General J. M., statute 137
Hopkins, Johns, residence 23
Hopkins Place 137
Howard, William 97
Howard Street 48, 66, 67, 90
Hucksters v, 63
Hume, Nelson 84
Hunting 130, 131

148

Ice skating 26, 133
Iron grillwork 76, 77
Iula, Bob 102
Jackson, Howard W. 25, 93, 94
Johns Hopkins Hospital 110-114
Johns Hopkins University 107
Johnson, Gerald W. 99
Jones, costumers 78
Jones Falls Expressway 147
Jousting 134
Katherine May 52
Kent, Frank R. 103
Kouwenhoven, Dr. W. B. 113
Kramer, Reuben 101
Krick, Perna 101
Lacrosse 135
Lamour, Dorothy 97
Latrobe, F. C. 53
Lazarus, Esther 95
Lehman, J. H. 84
Lexington Street 20, 47, 48, 62, 139
Liberty Street 20, 21, 47
Light Street 4, 5, 11
Locomotives 34, 58, 59
Loden, D. J. 92
Logan Field 37
Lombard Street 17, 63
Longshoremen 9, 80
Love Point Ferry 52
Lovejoy, Dr. Arthur O. 109
Lovely Lane Methodist Church 116
Manhattan, S.S. 55
Marie, Queen of Roumania 38
Markets
    Broadway 13
    Hollins 12, 65
    Lexington 62
    Lombard Street 17, 63
    Marsh 11
Martin aircraft 36, 41, 45
Martin, Glenn L. 96
Maryland Club 88
Maryland Hunt Cup 129
Maryland Institute 118, 119

McCollum, Dr. Elmer V. 108
McKeldin, Theodore R. 94
Memorial Stadium 133, 136
Mencken, August 98
Mencken, H. L. 98
Mencken, Sara H. 98
Migrant workers 45
Miller, J. Jefferson 140
Minnie 27
Montgomery Street v, 73
Motorcycling 132
Mt. Royal Avenue 118
Mt. Royal Railroad Station 119
Mt. Vernon Place 120, 121
Native Dancer 127
New Deal Barber Shop 71
Night Shift 39
O'Conor, Herbert R. 94
Orangeville Yard 34
Oyster boat 7
Painted screens 74
Patapsco River x, 30
Patterson Park 122
Peabody Institute Library 99
Pikesville Arsenal 19
Pimlico Race Track 124-126
Pleasant Street 22
Ponselle, Rosa 102
Pratt Street 4, 5, 21, 43, 56
Pressman, Hyman 94
Racing 124-129
Railroads 34, 58, 59, 69
Randolph, U.S.S. 55
Rationing 46, 47
Read Street Festival 122
Redwood Street 35
Rembski, Stanislav 101
Ring-around-a-rosie 15
Rivers Chambers Orchestra 31
Roosevelt, Franklin D. 38
Roland Park 18
Rowhouses 72-77
Ruperti, J. A. H. 85
Sagamore Farms 127

St. Leo's Carnival 17
Saratoga Street 23, 47
Savannah, N. S. 55
Schools 104-107, 115-119
Schmidt, Bill 83
Shakespeare Street 72
Shot Tower iii
Skinny-dipping 2
Smith, H. A. 83
Smith's Book Store 67
Smokey Joe 52
Snow scenes 1, 21, 26, 86
Soccer 135
State Window Cleaning 64
Stoop Sitting 16
Straw Hats 79
Street cars 20, 21, 24, 58, 69, 139
Sudhoff, Dr. Karl 111
Sun Building, The 138
Swimming 2, 29
Taussig, Dr. Helen B. 112
Thames Street x, 13, 66
Timonium State Fair 128
Tolchester 30
Tough Kids 65
Towson Hotel 23
Turnbull, Grace H. 101
Tyson Street 70
University of Maryland 115
V.E. and V.J. Days 48, 49
Vane Bros. Co. 56
War Memorial in the Snow 86
Washington Monument i
Watermelon Fleet 6, 7
Watermelon Man v
Watson, Arthur R. 123
Welch, Dr. W. H. 111
Welsh's Restaurant 65
Westport 79
White Steps 74
Windsor, Duke and Duchess of 97
Wiseman, William J. 90
Wood, Dr. Robert W. 108
Yardley, Richard Q. 103

Inner Harbor Renewal—an impression

ACKNOWLEDGEMENTS

The idea for this book was broached to Mrs. A. Aubrey Bodine shortly after she deposited her husband's negatives in the Peale Museum late in 1971. She enthusiastically approved the project, and was very helpful to us as we carried it forward. Nancy Bodine was Aubrey's favorite model, and by my choice, not hers, she can be found in pictures on pages 66 and 68. Incidentally, Seeber K. Bodine, the photographer's brother, is one of the two quail hunters on page 131.

Bodine's Baltimore did not become feasible until I had examined the entire collection of negatives. This was done in the summer of 1972, and at the same time they were carefully catalogued by Miss Barbara Borenstein under my supervision. That fall Mrs. Louis M. Kann, Jr. volunteered as editorial assistant and gave many hours of her time helping me winnow the material and plan the book's content. She also did picture research, advised me on the text, and compiled the index. Frances Kann's enthusiasm, knowledge of Baltimore and good taste contributed greatly to the quality of the book.

Harold A. Williams, editor of the *Sunday Sun* and Bodine's biographer, was a basic resource for information; he also read the text and made wise suggestions. Clement G. Vitek, chief librarian of the *Sun,* and his staff were generous with their time in helping our research, and the Maryland Department of the Enoch Pratt Free Library was a rich mine of information. Mrs. John Howard Eager did accurate research for a number of the pictures, and a great many other people supplied clues and tips which were useful in solving the puzzles. The manuscript was typed by Miss Ellen M. Engel, museum secretary.

The art director and designer of the book was Stanley Mossman. Some of the pictures were reproduced from original prints made by Aubrey Bodine, but most of the prints were made from Bodine's negatives, both film and glass plate, by Arthur Johnson of B/L Labs, Inc. Stanley L. Cahn of Bodine & Associates was not only an efficient editor, but a major contributor to the book's character through his extensive knowledge of Baltimore and of Bodine. My association with the production staff was both pleasant and rewarding.

Finally, I dedicate this book to Lucille whose encouragement and good advice made the long process from start to finish easier than it might have been.

Wilbur Harvey Hunter

Baltimore, July 1973

PRODUCTION NOTES

Design by Stanley Mossman
Typography by Modern Linotypers, Inc.
Text paper is Mohawk Vellum
Plates by Universal Lithographers, Inc.
Printed by Vinmar Lithographing Co.
Binding by Maple Press Company